Career Management

Secrets

The experts tell all!

About the author
Carolyn Boyes MA (Hons), DCH has been a trainer and coach for over a decade. She is the author of *Communication*, also in the **business secrets** series, and other books published by Harper Collins, including *Cool Careers, Need to Know? NLP* and *Need to Know? Cognitive Behavioural Therapy*.

Career Management
secrets

Collins

A division of HarperCollins*Publishers*

77-85 Fulham Palace Road, London W6 8JB

www.BusinessSecrets.net

First published in Great Britain in 2010 by HarperCollins*Publishers*
Published in Canada by HarperCollins*Canada*. www.harpercollins.ca
Published in Australia by HarperCollins*Australia*. www.harpercollins.com.au
Published in India by HarperCollins*PublishersIndia*. www.harpercollins.co.in

1

ISBN 978-0-00-732443-9

Printed and bound at Clays Ltd, St Ives plc

Contents

Learn how to manage your career

Most people fall into a career by accident. They might enjoy success or find themselves stuck in a job that's not fulfilling. By contrast, if you manage your career you take control of what you do, whether that's climbing the corporate ladder, starting your own business or perhaps going part-time.

I have spent more than a decade helping people all over the world decide what to do with their lives. Many of the people I coach have already worked for years, and some are just starting out. Surprisingly, it doesn't seem to matter what age people are, or where they come from or how successful they have been. Most people face the same sort of issues in trying to decide what to do next. They generally haven't spent enough time focusing on what work suits them best, what their long and short term goals might be and how best to put these into action.

Even some of those who are successful know some of the **secrets** but forget others. I am no different. I had a successful first career in international business before making a career change, and I had to find out many of these **secrets** for the first time. That's why you will find 50 **secrets** here, divided into seven easy-to-follow chapters:

■ **Take control.** Suggests that you step back and take a look afresh at who you are and what's important to you.

■ **Dare to dream.** How to create goals that are right for you.

■ **Be a rising star.** Lets you into the secrets of how to get promoted and rise within an organization.

■ **Market yourself.** Shows the importance of making yourself known in your career in order to achieve what you want.

■ **Create a life balance.** Helps you explore what to do if stress is getting to you and you want a change.

■ **Be ready for change.** Gives you key pointers for any successful career change. If you want to change or are forced to change careers this is what to do next.

■ **Be entrepreneurial.** Explains what will make you successful if you decide to leave paid employment and start up on your own.

If you follow these seven chapters of **secrets**, you will know how to manage your career sucessfully.

Create an achievable career plan and you are already on your way to a well-managed career for the rest of your life.

Take control

Start your career management by getting to know yourself. Applying the secrets in this first chapter will allow you to take a step back and think about not only what you are good at but also what motivates you. You can use this knowledge at every stage of your career to plan your next steps.

1.1

Be an entrepreneur

Do you take responsibility for your career or do you let your career just happen to you? In the old way of doing things you would leave school or university and expect to have a job for life. But with a changing world you need to stop and take stock.

The world is changing so rapidly now that there is no guarantee you will have a job for life, nor that the company you join will continue to exist, nor even that your industry will still exist in the next decade or so. There is only one thing you can do in a world like this, and that is to be an entrepreneur.

Entrepreneurs assume that they will have to make their own fortune (and I mean fortune in the sense of both luck and money). Entrepreneurs don't *let* things happen to them, they *make* things happen for them. This can be expressed by an equation: **cause > effect**.

one minute wonder Take a step back. Think about where you are in your career right now. Decide to make your career successful and fulfilling every day. You are in charge.

"The greatest discovery of my generation is that a human being can alter his life by altering his attitude of mind" William James, psychologist

■ **On which side of the equation are you?** Do you *cause* the situations you are in or are you generally at the *effect* of what other people do? Are you an *entrepreneur* or are you *passive*?

■ **Decide for yourself.** You can use the equation *cause* > *effect* as a reminder to take responsibility for your career decisions.

The self-employed are entrepreneurs. Every day, they take responsibility for making their careers as successful as possible. On the other hand, many employees of both large and small companies fall into the habit of being passive. They turn up to work on time and assume that as long as they do everything adequately, then their working lives will continue at an even pace, and they will always be paid until 30 or so years later the career comes to a close.

In the new world of rapid change this isn't enough. Every employee needs to be 'at cause' for their career.

You need to think like an entrepreneur if you want to make the right kind of progress in your career.

1.2

Take a personal inventory

One of the first things you can do to get on track in your career is take a personal inventory. This means looking at what you are really good at. Include not only your work skills and knowledge but also your natural talents and personal strengths.

The most thorough way to do this is to list each job role or activity you've carried out in the past and analyse each in turn. Think about the skills you used as well as any knowledge you gained. You will probably identify certain skills that you use consistently more than others.

case study The first job Sally had was in insurance. She had to deal with numbers and information all day long. She was bored and constantly passed over for promotion. Sally spent 10 years thinking she would never have much of a career. Then her company went through hard times and her job was made redundant. Sally took the opportunity to take

Next, look at the broad areas below. How do you rate your own skills in each of the areas: above average – good – average – below average? Write down the results.

■ **People.** For example, influencing people, persuading, supporting, helping, negotiating with, selling to, entertaining or teaching them.

■ **Ideas.** Being innovative, experimental, visionary or creative; being able to think well in the abstract, about future possibilities; how to change things for the better or improvise, design.

■ **Things.** For example, manual work, dealing with machinery or equipment, using tools, having practical skills.

■ **Data.** For example, handling details of numbers or information, interpreting and presenting data, IT, organizing and administrating.

Compare your list of the skills you have used in the past to the list of what you are good at. You can then make a new list combining the two: what you are good at and what you have experience in. This gives you an inventory of the strengths you will be selling in your career.

Find out whether you are naturally better with people, ideas, things or data.

a hard look at her skills and experience. She took a psychometric test, which confirmed that she needed a job focused on people. Now she works in a small company doing direct sales. "My biggest skill is in talking to people," she says. "I feel much happier and I have been so successful that I was promoted after a year!"

1.3

Discover your STARs

What have you done in your career so far? What have you done that you are proud of? An achievement is something you have undertaken with a result attached. If you know what's worked for you in the past, you can create more of the same type of achievement in the future and form a focused vision for your career.

The word achievement can sound quite scary to a lot of people. They tend to say, "I haven't achieved anything" because an achievement sounds as if it should describe something huge like climbing Everest or becoming CEO of a company. But of course you have achieved lots of things, in your work life and in your personal life.

one minute wonder Gain insight about what you value through your achievements. Look at each achievement and ask: "What is it about this achievement that is important to me?" If there isn't anything important, then decide not to do more of this type of work. If all your valuable achievements are in your personal life then maybe your work is lacking, so stop and pay heed.

An achievement is simply an action you have taken with a successful ending. There is a very simple way of remembering it: the **STAR** format. Try writing this down.

■ **S = Situation.** Think of a situation you have been in at work. Describe it in detail on your piece of paper.
■ **T = Task.** What was the task you were given to do in this situation or what was the responsibility you chose to take on?
■ **A = Action.** An achievement isn't something that is passive. What was the action you took to carry out this task? Did you organize? Lead? Administer? Calculate? Sell? Persuade?
■ **R = Result.** What was the positive result or benefit? Did it save money? Help people? Support a team? Make things more efficient?

Use your career achievements to work out your skills (also known as competencies). Take an achievement and write down what skills you used to get the result e.g. communication, leadership, teamworking. Which skills do you use most?

To understand yourself better, start making a list of at least one achievement from every part of your career so far. It will help you to develop a list of your key skills. Remember, you can always transfer your skills from one job to another.

Use the STAR format to write down your achievements and work out what you do well.

1.4

Discover your three Ps

It's no point being fantastic at your job if you hate it. You may make a reasonable career but you will lack any joy in what you do. The ingredients that make a career both fun and successful are Passions, Purpose and Principles. Get to know what yours are and make sure you include them in your career plan.

Your **Passions** are the things you love doing, that interest you and bring joy into your day. The quickest way to discover your Passions are to make three lists:

■ A list of the activities you need to have on a daily basis to make you feel satisfied.

■ A list of the activities you ideally like to have on a daily basis but which aren't essential.

■ A list of the activities you definitely *don't* want if you are to keep passionate about your career.

Your **Purpose** is the sense of fulfilment you get from your career when you are on track. You know you are fulfilling your purpose when you feel you are 'doing the right thing', and what you are 'really in business to do'. Think about what really gives meaning to your career to discover your purpose.

Your **Principles** are the third p. These are the ethical and moral standards that you need to abide by to feel ok about your career. For example if you are a vegetarian but forced to work with meat then you won't be working according to your principles. When you honour your principles you feel good about your career and feel it fits into how you want to live your life as a whole.

"You know you are on the road to success if you would do your job, and not be paid for it" **Oprah Winfrey**

The three Ps are Passion, Purpose and Principles. Identify yours.

1.5

Carry out your own 360

A 360-degree report is a tool used in business whereby an employee gets feedback on their performance from a variety of colleagues and clients, ranging from their boss to people below them. It is called a 360 because it gives a full range of views and a rounded sense of your performance and strengths and skills.

You don't have to wait until your company offers you this opportunity. Carry out your own informal 360 to understand how other people see you in a work situation. It's easy to do, and you can do it whether you are currently working or not.

one minute wonder A very effective question to set people thinking on your behalf is, "If there is one thing I could do to improve my chances of progressing my career, what would you advise?"

> **"A successful life is one lived through understanding and pursuing one's own path, not chasing after the dreams of others"**
>
> **Chin-Ning Chu, Business Author**

■ **Pick a handful of people.** They should know you well and come into contact with you on a regular basis. Up to ten is enough and ideally more than five.

■ **Ask for honest opinions.** Ask if they would be willing to answer some basic questions for you. The key is that you ask them to be honest and that you stay open and don't be defensive so that they feel they can say what really needs to be said.

■ **Keep things objective.** A good way to extract objective and honest advice is simply to ask if they have any specific examples of what you do well already as well as any areas you could improve. The more specific they are, the easier you will find it to act on their advice. If you are not clear what they mean, ask them, and again be open. Remember this is feedback, not criticism.

Take the feedback without being defensive and you will become aware of your potential weak areas as well as your strengths.

Ask people who know you well for feedback on your strengths, weaknesses and what you could do to be more effective.

Dare to dream

Career success is sometimes attributed to luck. But like any journey in life, you won't get where you want to go without both a goal and a plan. The secret of career management is knowing exactly what career suits you in the first place. Take what you know about yourself – your strengths, character, passions and principles – and match them up with a vision for your future.

2.1

Be visionary

Having a long-term vision for your career gives you focus. It helps you to come up with short term goals and plan your longer term career as well as respond positively to opportunities that come your way.

A study in the 1970s in America asked students about their future goals. Only a tiny percentage had a vision of their future over the coming years and an even smaller percentage had written their goals down. Years later the researchers returned and discovered that those students who had written down their goals had achieved more material and career success than all the other students put together.

Goals start with a big vision. What are the things you want to do, be and have in your career? Let your mind roam free and brainstorm some ideas.

one minute wonder Look to the past for clues to the future. Come up with three to five times in your life when you felt totally successful. Write them down. Describe what you did that made you succeed and what made you feel successful. What could you add into your vision?

"The future you see is the future you get"

Robert G Allen, author of One Minute Millionnaire

■ **Do a 'brain dump'.** Write down all the job options you have ever considered. Now rank them in order of desirability.

■ **Think about the skills and knowledge you enjoy using.** What industries and jobs use these?

■ **Create your ideal day.** Who would be involved? What would you do? How would it begin? Where would you go?

■ **Design your perfect environment.** Where would you be? What people would you have around you?

■ **Consider lesses and mores.** What could you do in future to create less of what you don't want and more of what you do want in your life?

Spend time doing this and ideas start to flow. Think way out into the future. Where do you want to be in your career 20 years from now or 30 years from now?

Don't censor yourself when you first want to do this. Think about all the things you would be proud to achieve in your career. The only limitations are ones you've created in your mind. Ok, you can't be an Olympic champion diver at 80 probably, but many other visions are feasible and therefore potentially achievable.

Give yourself a vision and it will provide a focus point for you to guide your whole career.

2.2

Be SMART

Having set a big vision for your future, you can start breaking it down into goal or outcomes. Decide your short and long term goals and make them SMART.

Breaking your vision down into smaller goals means that you can use them as milestones over the coming years. This makes your goals achievable. SMART goals are:

■ **S = Specific.** What you want specifically. Be as detailed as possible. Where, when, how, and with whom do you want this?

■ **M = Measurable.** How will you know when you have reached your goal? What is going to be your evidence of success?

■ **A = Achievable.** What actions will you need to take to achieve these goals? Give them more time? Gain more resources?

one minute wonder A great starting point when you first set your goals is to ask. "How is it possible that I don't have it now?" If you want it so much what is it that you need to do or change to get it? This question will throw up very useful answers.

"Think not of yourself as the architect of your career but as the sculptor" BC Forbes

■ **R = Realistic.** What makes these goals possible and probable? Do you need to change anything?
■ **T = Timed.** If you attach a time to your goals it will make you much more focused on taking action.

Have a guess at when you would expect to reach those outcomes: six months, one year, two years, 10 years, 20 years? The ideal situation is to end up with a balance of long and short term goals.

Pick out the four most important goals for you this year. Write down why you absolutely *will* achieve them. Be clear, concise and positive. Tell yourself why you're sure you can reach those outcomes and why it's important that you do.

What will your goals allow you to do? Think about what purpose they serve. What will you gain or lose if you achieve them? It takes effort to take action over a long period of time. Are you willing to make sacrifices in other parts of your life?

Remember that goals have to be really desirable and compelling, otherwise you are more likely to give up early.

Make sure your goals are SMART, which means specific, measurable, achievable, realistic and timed.

2.3

Step forth

A plan is great, but nothing can happen unless you take the first step, and then another. What are some things you can do today, this week, this month, this year to produce the results? Every journey, however long, starts with a single step.

Having set yourself some goals, the secret is to start taking action as quickly as possible on them. Identify your first steps.

1 Ask yourself, what is the gap between your current situation and what you want to achieve? Will it take training, discipline, study? What would you have to do first to accomplish each goal?

case study Ben decided on a 10-year goal for his career. The first actions he took were to write down details of what he wanted to achieve in terms of his qualifications, job title and degree. He also made a list of the skills, attitudes and beliefs he would need to have in order to achieve what he wanted. Then he made a list of how he had sabotaged himself in

> **"**Strong, deeply rooted desire is the starting point of all achievement**"** **Napoleon Hill, author of Think and Grow Rich**

2 Now decide on the smallest action that can immediately commit you to your plan. Is it applying for a course? Ringing a friend for information? Writing your CV?

It doesn't matter if you don't have a complete plan and some of your later steps are a little hazy when you start out to achieve your new career vision. You can fill in the later steps as you go on in your career. The important thing is to commit to heading off in the right direction. If necessary, you can always revise some of the milestones along the way.

Think of a first step you could take immediately for each goal.

the past and what he could do to solve these patterns of behaviour. Because the job he wanted was in a different work area, he also asked his boss if he could do some work shadowing in another department in order to gain some new skills. This gave him valuable experience with direct relevance to his long-term goal.

2.4

Commit 100%

Nobody can make things happen by being passive. It is no good setting wonderful goals without doing anything about them. Equally it is pointless just doing one thing. Spending a lot of time getting to know what you want will help you commit 100% to going after what you want to achieve.

To grow your career you will sometimes need to move a little or perhaps a lot outside your existing comfort zone. This is because you need to be experimental and try new things in order to create new experiences and new successes in your life.

■ **An attitude of total commitment**. Prepare to be flexible, take risks and stick your neck above the parapet.

one minute wonder Bear in mind the saying: "There is no failure, only feedback." If you stretch yourself you will make some mistakes but these don't matter. When you don't get the result you want, use what you learn to make better choices next time that will move you towards your goals.

"The victory of success is half won when one gains the habit of setting goals and achieving them"

Og Mandino, author of The Greatest Salesman in the World

■ **The will to change.** Committing to goals may mean you have to be the person who is willing to go out and learn a new skill. It may make you the person who is willing to shoulder the responsibility for a task or who gets up early and works an extra hour to achieve what you really want.

Think through what you really need to do to get your goal. If you aren't willing to do what it takes (and I mean *whatever* it takes), you may achieve something but probably not what you originally intended. You won't be managing your career as such and you'll be back at the effect side of the cause > effect equation.

Of course you are allowed to change your goals. So if you get halfway to your promotion or to setting up a new company or retraining for a new job and think, "No this isn't right for me anymore", then it's ok to have a different goal. But if you do want your goal, you need to commit to it, not 99% or even 99.95. It's going to take 100% focus and energy to see you through.

But remember if you have the right goal, the rewards at the other end will be worth the wait.

Only 100% commitment will put you in control of achieving meaningful goals.

2.5

Find a role model

No one is going to have exactly the same goals as you, but there may be people who have taken a similar path or who you can regard as role models. Even if you don't know them personally, you can still take inspiration from what others have done.

What resources do you have now? What resources do you need for your projected outcome? Perhaps you have a certain amount of knowledge but you know you lack other skills.

For example, suppose you want to get a promotion. Have you ever had or done this before? What skills did you use? Networking? Negotiation? If you have done something before, you have a reference point for what works and what doesn't. If you take similar actions you will probably get similar results.

But supposing you have never had the kind of career success that you want to achieve now. How can you identify and gain the skills you need? Well, you can either start from scratch or you can learn from what has and hasn't worked for your role models.

1 Do you know anyone who has successfully risen to the sort of position you want to be in? Do you know this person well enough to ask them about their experience? If they are senior within your company could you ask them to mentor you or coach you?

2 What resources do you imagine you will need to fulfil your goal? Think about your role model. What resources did they draw upon to achieve what they wanted? Is there anything similar you could go out and get that would help you?

3 If there is no obvious person in your life who could perform this role for you, then look around. Have you seen anyone on television or elsewhere, either in your own country or abroad, who you can emulate or learn from? What do you imagine they would advise you to do as a next step?

Learn from role models you know personally or from public life.

Market
yourself

The ability to market yourself is a vital career management skill. Most roles inside and outside your organization are probably not advertised. Your chances of promotion may depend on the contacts you make and the strength of your reputation. How can you best sell yourself to employers?

3.1

Brand yourself

How do you want to define what value you bring to an employer? Think about your USP – your Unique Selling Point. This is marketing jargon used to describe the features of a product that make it valuable and different from other products on the market. What is distinctive and valuable about you?

Think about some of the top brands in the world. They all have something special we associate them with. What comes into your mind when you hear the names Ferrari, Shell, HSBC, Qantas Airlines, for example? It might be reliability, efficiency, value for money, glamour or excitement perhaps. Large companies spend a fortune making sure they sell consistent messages about what values they represent, and that's one

case study Joe was working for several years in a large financial company managing a small team and specializing in documentation. He wanted to progress but found there was little demand for documentation specialists. He then decided to redefine his job title on his CV. Instead of calling

of the reasons they are so successful. These messages are their brand, and the message which stands out most is the unique selling point. What's yours?

■ **You are unique.** It doesn't matter what kind of career you have, you bring meaning and passion to a job based on your unique combination of interests, values, experience, ambitions and vision.

■ **You are a brand.** Your brand is the elements of yourself that you choose to promote openly. So, for example, maybe you are very structured and organized with a background working in charities and business, and at the same time you are creative and innovative.

■ **You can market yourself.** To which aspects do you want to draw employers' attention? If you were a product and selling yourself with an advertising slogan or a one-liner, what would you want to say about yourself? If you could only choose one thing about yourself that your employers should notice that makes you really special, what would it be?

Once you know your USP, you can go out and sell yourself, on your CV and around your company.

Think of yourself as a unique brand that brings value to an organization.

himself a documentation specialist, he gave himself a broader label (changing his brand) – a professional manager. Soon he found that agents were putting him forward for jobs that he hadn't been considered for before. He eventually found a new role in the retail sector.

3.2

Leave a lasting impression

A brand is only effective if it is well communicated. What is it about good communicators that leaves a lasting impression? How do they always seem to say the right things in the right way?

There are three ways to communicate. The things that you say, the voice you say them in, and the body language you use.

1 You might think that **what you say** is the most important part of the message you want to get across to other people but it's not at all. Research has shown that in fact only 7 per cent of our message is down to the words that we use.

one minute wonder Here's an immediate step you can take to gain flexibility with your voice. Take a couple of deep breaths through the nose. Inhale all the way down to your stomach and exhale. Practise reading aloud a paragraph from a book and notice how your voice begins to sound less constrained and more relaxed.

> **"It's not what you know but who you know that makes the difference"** **Anonymous**

2 A huge 55 percent of communication is in **body language** – the gestures we use, facial expressions and how we stand or sit. From this, other people know whether you have self confidence, whether you are authoritative and whether you believe in what you are saying. If you use powerful words but you don't really believe the words you say, this will 'leak' into your body language.

3 The remaining percentage of our communication – over a third – is in the **voice**. Your feelings show up in how deeply you breathe and how relaxed you are, which feeds through to your voice. If you are breathing shallowly your voice will sound tight and higher than if you breathe deeply. People will also pick up on your accent, the tone of your voice and whether you emphasize some words more than others.

Look at great speakers of our age to see how they make an impact. President Obama, for example, is widely considered to be a strong orator – he delivers speeches with an erect body posture and a calm and controlled pattern of speech.

Control your body language and voice to make a lasting impression.

3.3

Have an elevator pitch

Being able to introduce yourself succinctly and articulately is a vital part of self-marketing. It is useful in informal networking situations and in formal interviews. You are always on show in your career, whether within your company or at an external conference or business meeting.

■ **What is an elevator pitch?** An elevator pitch is a term used to describe the succinct speech an entrepreneur gives to describe his product or company. The 'elevator' part comes from the idea that the speech could be delivered within the time it takes to ride from ground floor up to top floor in an elevator.

■ **Why do I need an elevator pitch?** Whenever you meet somebody, wherever you are, you should seek to make as good an impression as you would in a formal interview. You never know when a chance meeting could turn into an interview.

■ **How long have I got?** You should be able to introduce yourself succinctly; which means within a duration of minimum 30 seconds up to a maximum of one minute. The idea is not that you speak really fast and boast about yourself, but that you describe yourself in an interesting manner to other people.

one minute wonder Bear your short and long term career objectives in mind when you work out your elevator pitch. For example, you may want to find out about other jobs, companies or people to whom you can be referred, so you could include "I am currently trying to find out about..." in your pitch.

■ **How do I start?** First of all introduce yourself politely by saying who you are and what you do. This doesn't need to be an elaborate description. For example, "Hello, my name is … I currently work as an accountant at …"

■ **Then what?** Be prepared to be able to describe your strengths and skills. That's why it is important to have done your self-analysis and assessment first before getting out and talking to people. You may well be asked even in a casual way something like, "Oh, what do you specialize in?", or "How interesting, what kind of nursing?"

Think about what it is you really want to get across about yourself in a first meeting. For example, "I'm someone who loves detail and getting into the nitty gritty of information" or "I'm in IT, but I really specialize in designing websites for creative people."

Always keep what you say brief to keep the other person interested. Write down some key points in advance of going out and talking to people and practise, practise and practise again.

Always be ready to say something interesting about yourself in less than a minute.

3.4

'Act as if'

Have you ever watched someone nervous giving a presentation? Body language all over the place, sweating, tripping over words, possibly even apologizing as well. It's not enjoyable to be around. Change the scenario. What's it like to be around someone confident? Who are you more likely to buy from? Person One or Two?

■ **Confidence is attractive and sexy.** (By the way, I mean confidence, not arrogance, which is neither). We like confident people because they are more comfortable to be around. You may feel sorry for someone who is nervous or has low self esteem, but you are not going to buy their product or them.

one minute wonder Change your posture to instantly feel better about yourself. Practise standing with poise and balance. Relax your arms by your side. Let your head rest gently and evenly between your shoulders. If you stand well you will feel good.

■ Already confident? I imagine that at this point a lot of people say, "It's easy to be confident if you are." True, but there is a great trick to appearing confident. You can change the way you think about yourself or there's a quicker way, which is to act as if you are already confident.

■ It's an act. Think about standing in front of a group of people presenting. You can hunch up your shoulders and clasp your hands in front of your body and tell yourself how scared you feel. Or you can be a Hollywood star for the day and put on a show. If I were an actor giving a performance in which I played a great presenter, how would I act? I would probably stand with very straight posture, calmly breathing and exuding quiet authority. In other words, pretending.

■ Now it happens for real. The strange thing is that by pretending to be confident, you really do change the way you feel. You genuinely start to exude confidence because you feel more confident and then it becomes a habit. Soon you can't stop yourself, and you'll exude confidence everywhere, all over the office in everything you do. Then other people will start to notice and you might get picked up for all sorts of opportunities.

Pretend to feel confident and you will soon find yourself coming across to others as if you are.

In fact, this is such a powerful secret, only do it if you really want to grow your career.

3.5

Maintain a broad network

Successful people have one thing in common. Whatever their career, they are not struggling alone. They have wide networks inside work and also outside work and they know not only how to build a strong network but also how to leverage it. The good thing is that you can learn how to do this too, no matter where you are in your career.

■ **What's the point of networking?** There is a relationship between success and good networking skills. Successful people understand that it's other people who will help them find jobs and be promoted, and they see the time spent on networking as an investment rather than a distraction from their business. If you want to get your career going make sure you schedule time in for networking and also have it as an important part of your daily life at work and at home.

■ **Natural networking.** Networking doesn't mean just going to professional meetings and giving your business card to someone. Networking is what happens naturally every time you meet someone.

■ **Cast a wide net.** A network means far more than nurturing a few influential, well-established friends. In fact, the key to successful net-

"I am bound to everyone on this planet by a trail of six people"

Frigyes Karinthy

working is that the broader your web of contacts, the better. You don't have to be very close to someone to benefit. Research shows that weak relationships can still act as a bridge to other people just as effectively as strong relationships.

■ **The network potential.** Anybody can recommend you in your career from a friend to a work colleague to your hairdresser. The reason broad networking works is because of six degrees of separation, also known as the human web. This is the well-researched theory of Hungarian author Frigyes Karinthy: that anyone in the world is separated by just six steps from anyone else they want to meet.

■ **Use the human web to spread your reputation.** Whether you are looking for information or a referral, ask people you know. You may not know the right person immediately, but the people you meet know people who know people. If you are always clear about what you do, then your network will market you.

A broad, loose network is better than a small tight network for creating opportunities in your career.

3.6

Create a buzz

Getting yourself a name for what you do inside your chosen industry is a great career enhancer. It will make you contacts, give you development opportunities in your career and ultimately find you jobs before they are advertised, making sure your name is the first one to be considered.

1 Make yourself visible in your industry. Join the professional bodies, volunteer to help out at conferences, be ready to speak on your subject or just keep in touch with the latest industry news by signing up for newsletters and talks.

case study Mei Li says: "I never used to join in with groups because I felt intimidated going to places where I didn't know anyone. Now I make a real effort to talk to everyone from the waiters to the VIPs. I have discovered that even people who aren't directly in my profession can be helpful, like the wife of my now boss. It was only because we started

2 At conferences and meetings, don't just speak with the people you already know. Look at the list of attendees ahead of time. Introduce yourself or ask someone you know to introduce you. Make sure you remember the names of everyone you meet, and have your elevator pitch ready.

3 Take every opportunity to build your network of professional contacts not just by asking for help but by offering to help. There's always something you can do for another person, however small, whether it is information or a contact name.

4 Ask questions and stay interested. Forget about "what's in it for me", and instead find a real point of connection with everyone you talk to, whether it's about work, hobbies or the meeting. Remember to follow up and send that contact name or article they were looking for.

Always look for opportunities to help others, and you will soon make new friends across the industry.

chatting that I heard her husband had a job going. I sent her a note after the event saying how nice it was to meet her and hoping we would meet again, and she sent a note back to say that her husband would be interested in having a talk with me. I rang him up, we spoke briefly, and then a few weeks later I had a formal interview."

3.7

Link in for luck

The internet opens up a whole new world for networkers. Whether it is your own website or a social networking group, the internet helps you to promote yourself and make new contacts and connections. Make sure you give out a clear message online to maintain a consistent career brand.

Many job hunters are happy to use online job boards to look for work, and these can be very effective. However their usefulness goes as soon as you have landed the job. Networking sites or your own website will have a much longer shelf life for you and can create a great buzz around your career.

There are many different networking sites out there, some are for personal networking and some for professional networking. All of them can be useful in keeping track of who you know.

■ **LinkedIn.** The LinkedIn website (www.linkedin.com) is now seen by professionals and headhunters as one of the most popular online networking management tools for successful people in their career. The great thing about this kind of site is that people don't even need to know your name to find you – a search on a job title or company name may show you up.

> **"**More business decisions occur over lunch and dinner than at any other time, yet no MBA courses are given on the subject**"**

Peter Drucker, Business author

■ **Blogs, YouTube and Twitter.** If you are in a profession, it is worth considering having your own website or even maintaining a blog or podcast. Or if you really want to up your profile, how about a video on YouTube (www.youtube.com)? Or start 'twittering' (twitter.com).

■ **Facebook and MySpace.** If you use social networking sites like Facebook (www.facebook.com) or MySpace (www.myspace.com), make sure that your brand, or projected image, here is not in conflict with your brand on more professional networking sites. Be consistent in everything you do. The web is a potent tool.

Consider what messages show up first when someone does a search on your name. We are more and more visible on the web nowadays, so successful people take care to keep a clean brand on the web. If you have your own website, then colleagues and potential employers who are searching for you will probably find that first rather than a piece of information over which you have no control.

Use online networking sites to promote your image and personal brand.

3.8

Be visible inside your company

Successful employees have strong networks inside their own companies. However, sometimes employees see the idea of networking with colleagues as 'office politics' and quite a manipulative thing to do. In reality, effective networking is based on genuine interest in other people and genuine friendliness.

Networking in a company doesn't mean being a ruthless politician. It means cultivating relationships with your colleagues that are win-win and mutually helpful. How do you begin? Some of the steps you can take are very simple.

case study "I had always been a reluctant networker until recently", says Johann. "What changed my mind was when I got chatting to some people from another department. They told me about a technology problem they had, and I said I could pop over for five minutes to help. We always chatted by the

- **Open up informal conversations.** Don't just sit at your desk on the phone. Move round the office, smile to people and start chatting.
- **Listen.** Find out the concerns and goals of other people in your office. Get into work earlier and leave later so you have time to chat.
- **Be helpful.** If someone needs help outside your team or function, then be the person who does it and builds a good reputation.
- **Cut across functions.** If you have ideas and information that could help others, make sure you communicate them.
- **Be social.** Give up some of your free time to be with colleagues. Buy drinks, give birthday cards, go to office parties and don't get drunk.
- **Take a break.** Have lunch with other people, not at your desk.
- **Seize opportunities.** Go on courses or to meetings with other teams. If you attend a conference, then stay afterwards to chat.
- **Use your namecards.** At meetings and conferences give out two namecards, for someone to keep one and pass the other to someone else.
- **Ask for feedback.** Finally, ask your colleagues for feedback on how you are doing. Be open enough to invite comments.

So-called viral marketing uses word of mouth to promote a product. Use the same idea to make yourself visible within your company.

Spread the idea that you are both great at your job and a great human being.

coffee machine after that and I started playing squash with one of the guys every Thursday. I never thought of it as networking. Then one of them said he had told the boss of another department that I might be good as their IT guy. It shows you never know when impressions count."

3.9

Write it well

The ability to communicate in speech is going to make a huge difference in your career. However, even though the world of work is more casual than it used to be, being able communicate in writing is equally important. You need to put your points across in a professional way that supports what you say.

You may need to write emails or letters to colleagues, your boss or clients. At some stage in your career you will probably have to write some kind of covering letter to a future employer. Whatever you need to write, you will be judged on how well you do it. Here are some basics to bear in mind next time you put pen (or laptop) to paper.

case study Anish says: "I was having no luck sending my CV to employers until I changed my cover letter. I realized that it was so long, no one was bothering to read it. Most people only spend seconds reading the letter. Now I stick to a simple format. My starting paragraph says why I am applying for the job and where I found out about them. Paragraph two

■ **Get the basics right.** Make the typeface easy to read. Check for spelling mistakes and good grammar. You'd be amazed how many people send off a letter riddled with inaccuracies.

■ **Have a reason to write.** If you don't need to put it in writing, then don't. It might be better to communicate by talking instead.

■ **Be discreet.** If you don't want your email re-read or passed on to others, don't write it down to begin with.

■ **Know what you want to communicate.** Cut the waffle. If you make your points clearly you will leave a strong impression.

■ **Know your audience.** It may not be appropriate to write to your boss or a client in the same way as a friend. Be formal if in doubt.

■ **End with a follow up.** If you are writing a letter or email, what do you want to happen next? Make sure the reader knows how you are going to follow up.

Being a good written communicator sells you very effectively whether you are in a company or looking for a new job. As with everything else you do, it reinforces your reputation as a professional.

Only write something down if you really need to, and make it count.

says what I have to offer – it is a three-line summary of my main skills and experience. Then I say that I have attached my CV and am going to follow up with a phone call within a few days. So far it has worked every time. I don't have to ring; the employer actually reads my CV and contacts me to arrange an interview."

Be a rising star

To manage your career within a company you will need to make yourself promotable. Being the sort of person to whom others give responsibility opens up new opportunities for growth and development in your career. (It also ensures in tough times that you are the last person to face the sack.)

4.1

Align yourself with your organization

An employment contract isn't just a legal contract. Behind it lies another deal: an emotional contract. You, the employee, agree to give up your time and freedom to work for someone else in return for money, security and other daily needs.

This unspoken mutual contract works to everyone's benefit and happiness if your and your employer's needs are aligned. For example, perhaps I like to take on a challenge and seize every opportunity to learn, while my organization rewards people who take on challenges.

However what happens if I love being creative, and being with a team of relaxed people, but my employer values fast-paced, task-focused environments and puts my values second to his or her needs? When your needs are out of alignment with your organization's needs, you will start to feel unhappy, then your unhappiness may affect other people around you. You are unlikely to be promoted. Ultimately you might resign or even be fired.

If you can align yourself with your organization then you will have a high chance of growing your career within the same company and not have to make dramatic career changes.

■ **Goals.** What are your organization's goals? Check out the company mission statement if there is one. What can you contribute?

■ **Values.** What does your organization value in its employees? Think about not just what it says it values but also what behaviours/skills are rewarded.

■ **Needs.** Now think about your needs. How do the organization's needs fit with what you need in your career?

■ **Offer.** Is what you have to offer the organization (knowledge/experience) aligned with what they can offer you back in terms of reward?

■ **Change.** What would you have to do differently to align yourself? Is this something you can do happily?

If you can align yourself with your organization then you are going to happily take actions that have a positive impact for your organization. They will then reward you in your career.

Be clear about what you need in your career and what your organization values most in its employees.

4.2

Always deliver

At the early stages of your career, your employer buys you for your potential. The employer expects to have to train you, so you are evaluated on the basis of your personal qualities and character. As you carry on in your career, you will be employed and promoted on how efficiently you deliver results.

In business, the people who deliver most efficiently are those who work hard and also keep an eye on objectives. Think about these points:

1 To get yourself noticed and promoted will involve more than just fulfilling the tasks your manager asks you to carry out. Valuable people within an organization think about both the day-to-day tasks they are assigned and the needs of the wider organization. Your ability to keep your eye on delivering immediate and long term goals will set you above other employees.

2 Always be happy not only to do what someone asks of you but also to do more than is expected. If someone asks for a volunteer to shoulder responsibility, then be that volunteer. Sacrificing your time and energy will pay dividends later.

> **"In business, I've discovered that my purpose is to do my best to my utmost ability every day"**
>
> **Donald Trump, American businessman**

3 People who carry out tasks on time and within budget make themselves promotable. They find out what aspect of the task is important to their employer and make sure they fulfil the task not only within their own expectations but also within their employer's expectations.

4 This is not always the obvious thing: while some managers may want a task to be delivered within budget no matter who it affects, other managers may value the money side but equally want you to motivate your team sufficiently at the same time to support whatever you do wholeheartedly.

Deliver both your team's goals and your organization's goals and you will be valued throughout the company.

4.3

Be positive

In any business setting you are being judged for what you do and how you do it. Even if you think you are almost invisible in your job, someone will notice you. One of the first things that makes an impression is your attitude. Are you someone who whinges and gossips or are you professional and positive? Follow these three essential rules if you want to make progress.

1 **Don't be a gossiper.** It's good to be a team member and chat and join in social events. However, does that mean you have to drop down to the lowest level of gossipers? Of course not. Just because other people are complaining about how dreadful the boss is or how terrible the company treats its employees, don't be tempted to join in. Remember that you will be the boss one day. You will be heading up this company.

2 **Don't develop a 'them' and 'us' attitude.** Of course, you need to get on with your team members. Setting yourself apart and stating your ambitions too boldly isn't going to win you many friends. You won't be promoted if you don't fit in and have allies. So sure, be open to hearing what other people have to say. People love to have colleagues listen to their daily gripes. Just don't be tempted to fall in with 'them' and 'us' whinges about the people who hand out work to you. If you want to grow your career and be promoted you are going to need to become friendly with your future bosses and impress them just as much as your current colleagues.

3 **Have a 'can do' attitude instead.** You are far more likely to be seen positively if you are have a 'can do', positive attitude. Even when everybody else is fed up, over-worked and starting to flag, be the person who sees through the goal enthusiastically. Misery does tend to love company as the saying goes, so you might lose a few companions by being positive but you will replace them with many more successful and positive ones.

Recent research shows that the most optimistic people are also the luckiest people. If you have a positive attitude then you will believe you can accomplish more and therefore you will accomplish more.

Be positive and you will win over the people who matter.

4.4

Find a niche

In every team there's a really valuable person. He or she may not be the person who knows the business better than everyone else but they do something really well. Perhaps they are good at booking the office night out, or great at helping other team members write reports or knowing how to get round the system or tell great jokes.

They stand out because they do something for the team and the organization that no one else does. Moreover, it's something that goes above and beyond their job description. No one said when they joined that they needed to do any of these things but they provide in effect some kind of service for the team that makes things run more smoothly or more enjoyably. This may not seem very much on paper, but if you have ever been in a company where redundancies are on the cards then you'll notice these are the last people to go. They have their niche, and you need your own niche too.

■ **The niche must not be specific to the team.** Now you don't want your niche to be indispensable to your team's business because otherwise you will never get promoted. Your team will keep you there forever doing the same thing year after year.

■ **The niche needs to reach out to the broader network.** Your niche needs to be helpful and valuable (rather than vital), so that people in power notice what a great person you are and think, "I want that person in my team. They seem to be particularly helpful / good at writing / good with people etc."

■ **The niche needs to be social.** Your ideal niche should put you in contact with lots of people in the company. For example, you could become the person who buys the presents for those who are leaving, or shows colleagues how to use their new software more efficiently, or introduces everyone to a really useful website.

Before long, you will be on first name terms with different people and different teams and your boss's bosses will have noticed you. Then you are only one step away from: "What about so and so for this new job. They always seem reliable / a real team player / enjoyable to work with." If you are up against someone who hasn't carved a nice niche for themselves, then who is going to win the promotion?

You every time.

Create a niche for yourself so that everyone wants to work with you.

4.5

Become your own coach

In any career some things work out the way you want, and others don't. As the saying goes, it's not what happens to you that matters, it's how you react to what happens to you and what you do in response that makes the difference. Successful people learn from things that go wrong as well as right.

Careers aren't static. They aren't just lists of responsibilities. Every day you work you do things that have an impact on the people around you. They may have a positive impact or a negative one. You may be told off or hopefully praised. If you are going to grow your career, external feedback is useful but you need to be able to do without it and become objective about yourself. You need to become your own coach.

■ **What does a coach do?** A great coach helps you to know yourself – what you can do — your personal qualities and skills. Each time you do something they ask you to reflect back on it. What can you learn from what went right and what went wrong? This is true if you have not succeeded in the way you wanted to, but equally even if you went beyond your original expectations.

"When defeat comes, accept it as a signal that your plans are not sound, rebuild those plans, and set sail once more toward your coveted goal**"**

Napoleon Hill, American author

■ **Reflect on your mistakes and successes.** Looking at your mistakes makes sure you don't repeat them and gets you to stretch yourself outside your comfort zone. Reflecting on your successes ensures you repeat them again and again. What is it that you do that makes the difference? What is it that you do that other people don't do?

Being your own coach trains you to take full ownership of your future successes. You will not only learn and develop as a person, but also bring much more joy and enthusiasm into your daily working life.

Self-coaching will build your confidence and make you aware of your strengths and weaknesses.

4.6

Keep career records

I often see people who have been working for 15 years and want to change jobs. They look wonderful on their CVs but have very little confidence. "I haven't really done anything in my career", they say. "I just got on with my job and I haven't achieved anything." Or, "I do my job, but I haven't got any particular skills."

When you've been in a job for a while, it's easy to become complacent and think you will never have to look for a new job or sell yourself again. As such, you might forget to keep track of your achievements. However, it is a very useful exercise to keep career records.

one minute wonder Each time you review your career records, ask yourself: "Am I on track to my goals? Do I need to change anything in my current role? Do I need any additional resources? Is what I am doing visible to others in the company? Am I getting career satisfaction from this?

"I've always worked very, very hard, and the harder I worked, the luckier I got" Alan Bond, Australian businessman

■ **Keep a running record of achievements.** You will not only be well-prepared if you change career but also able to explain easily what you do successfully to your current employers.

■ **Look at the gaps.** Even more than this though, if you keep track of what you do, you will start to notice any gaps in terms of your own professional development. If you are becoming a bit stale in your career, then now's your chance to fill the gaps before it's too late.

■ **Make it a regular assessment.** Why not keep a record of what you do on a monthly or quarterly basis just like you would keep an eye on your bank account? Have a running log in which you record any new skills you have gained, any projects you have completed or results you have achieved for the company.

■ **Include achievements outside of work.** After all, the skills in non-work interests can be just as useful.

■ **Be specific.** Make sure you note down dates, people involved and any commendations or positive comments you received.

You will find that regularly reviewing your work in this way keeps your mind focused and provides you with the ammunition to sell yourself far more effectively within the company.

Keep a record of your on-going skills and achievements.

4.7

Update your CV

Yes, Curriculum Vitae literally means 'life history' but it's not going to get you a job unless you hone it down. Your CV can be your best marketing document. Just like a marketing brochure, it is going to sell you specifically to your chosen target audience if you customize it and write it well.

1 **Use your career log to keep your CV updated.** You never know when you will need it. It needs to have details of your career history with dates attached. It should include your educational qualifications, professional training and professional associations. It should also always be honest and accurate.

2 **Tailor your CV to your career goals.** It helps enormously if you have networked and researched and made yourself clear about what people in your target role are likely to want to know about you. Your CV is going to operate as a door opener: a marketing brochure for potential openings in the company or outside; a means of getting to an interview; and also very possibly as the main agenda for the interview once you get there.

> **one minute wonder** Go and read your CV. Make sure it is filled with achievements, skills and proof of motivation. If it is not, then it needs a rewrite. Keep it short – two sides is ample.

3 **Write a profile at the top of your CV.** The best way to customize your CV is to include a summary at the start. This will be like your elevator pitch in introducing yourself in a succinct, sharp way. Keep it to about four lines, and explain what you do in words that are relevant and understandable to your audience.

4 **Contextualize yourself.** If you work as a secretary for a small business, state this. If you work in one of the world's biggest companies or have worked in several different sectors, then give this information clearly.

5 **Describe the breadth and depth of your experience.** In other words, the sort of areas you excel at as well as how many years you have worked in each area.

6 **Remember your Unique Selling Point.** Finally, include your USP and make sure it is relevant for the role you want.

Your CV can open doors for you if you treat it like a marketing brochure.

4.8

Sell your ideas

Your ability to communicate and influence others is indispensable to achieving your career goals. As Shakespeare said, "no man is an island". We all need support from other people, whether friends, colleagues or clients. The most effective people are those who persuade others to support their ideas.

Selling is not just for extrovert, aggressive, pushy business types. If you have ideas and goals, you will be infinitely more resourceful if you can enlist help and co-operation from other people to achieve them.

What doesn't work is trying to bulldoze through your ideas. What does work is being 'naturally' persuasive. Opposite are two secrets to being naturally persuasive.

one minute wonder Paint a mental picture in another person's head of what their life will be like when they have adopted your idea. Start by asking them to imagine a future scenario. Now contrast that with what they have now. If the future picture looks more appealing they will 'buy' into it.

"Understand that you need to sell you and your ideas in order to advance your career"

Jay Abraham, American marketing guru

1 **Understand that humans are motivated by need.** If you understand human nature, then you can sell your ideas. Some people are motivated to move towards something they want. At the very least we are all motivated by survival: we want our basic needs fulfilled: food, sleep and love. After these come individual needs, which are pleasurable if we have more of them, for example, friends, comfort, possessions, status, power.

2 **Offer more pleasure and less pain.** We are also often motivated to move away from what we don't want: pain or discomfort, being told off, lack of money, unpleasant surroundings. Persuasive people show others how achieving goals will bring more pleasure and less pain. "Let's get that project done by next week. If we are ahead of schedule we are all going to get a bonus." (Money / reward /pleasure.) "How about we talk to the boss about this problem now? If we leave it any later (s)he is going to be even angrier." (Avoid pain / anger.)

Learn to be persuasive and you will become a natural leader who other people rely on to set the pace and goals for them.

Offer people more pleasure and less pain if you want them to buy your ideas.

Strike a balance

Career management doesn't just mean having a career and letting the rest of your life fall apart: that was a 20th-century way of thinking. In the 21st century changes in the global employment market spurred on in part by technology have made it easier for flexible work patterns to become more normal.

5.1

Know your priorities

How well do you know your satisfaction levels in your life as a whole? Do you want to carry on working full time but work more at home? Would you prefer to work part time and free up time for other activities? Or perhaps work full time but different hours or different shifts?

These are some steps you can take immediately:

1 A good way to begin is to draw a circle on a piece of paper. Divide it into pie slices.

2 In each slice of the pie, write the name of an area of your life, for example, family, work, hobbies, personal development and friendships.

3 In the centre of the circle write the number one. On the outside of the circle write the number ten. Now think about how happy you are currently in each area of your life.

4 Rate each area between one and ten by drawing a line across the pie slice. For example, a line across the middle of your 'family' slice would equal five out of ten.

You will probably end up with some complete slices where you are very satisfied and some small slices where you are very dissatisfied.

■ Ask yourself, do you want the areas where you are less satisfied to have more priority in your life?
■ If so, what will you have to change elsewhere in your life to give more time and energy to the other areas?
■ If the answer lies in the balance of your work and the rest of your life, what aspects of your work do you need to change?

Knowing your priorities will make you more effective as a negotiator in your career and allow you to make choices that are right for you.

5.2

Get ready for risk

How much risk are you ready for? Knowing how comfortable you are with risk is very important before you make any kind of career move whether to another job or self employment. Will what you gain in your career in the short or the long term outweigh any personal or professional costs?

An acceptable level of risk for you may be very different than for others. Making a decision about the risks and benefits of a career move is easier if you follow these steps.

■ **List.** Draw up a list of the risks versus benefits of each option. Think about how big a career change you want. Are you changing jobs within the same industry? Or changing industries too?

case study Anthony says: "When I reached 50 years old, I decided that I didn't want to work night-shifts any more because my health had worsened and my doctor said I needed to look after my blood pressure. The company had no problem with my swapping to day shifts, but I realized even that wasn't

■ **Needs.** Consider your immediate and longer term goals and finances. Is it worth giving up income now for greater possibilities in the future?

■ **Back up.** Do you have a back up plan if it doesn't work out? Could you return to your previous job?

■ **Impact.** Consider how easy it will be to adapt to a new pattern of working hours. Who else in your life would be impacted?

Remember that trying to avoid risk may also backfire. In the 21st century some of the best placed people are not those who have taken the stable-looking path but those who have become entrepreneurs and control their own career destiny. You don't need to be self employed to be an entrepreneur.

You can think in this way even if you are employed by taking the same time to plan your career and the potential risks as if it were a business decision for your organization.

Do your research. Risks aren't always obvious. In the past, working for a bank would have been a very secure profession. Since the recession, though, big organizations can be as insecure as smaller ones.

Always be aware of the risk level you are prepared to live with in any career change.

enough. I really wanted to take a couple of days off a week and help out with my wife's catering business. I went back to my boss and we agreed that I could job share my role. He got two brains for the price of one, and I got two jobs for only slightly less money (and I sleep better too)."

5.3

Do it your way

Many employees don't find it easy to say no to job demands because they are afraid of the impact it will have on their career. However, you can't keep saying yes if you want to create a better balance between your career and the rest of your life. You need to be able to say no politely.

Are you going to say no to your partner: "I can't do that because I am working this weekend?", or no to your boss: "I can't work in this way any more?" If you think your work life balance would be better served by a non-traditional working pattern then it's time to sell the concept to your boss.

You have only two things to sell to an employer: **time** and **knowledge**.

one minute wonder Stop your 'shoulds'. There are a lot of 'musts', 'ought to' and 'shoulds' in organizations. Walk around a typical office and you will hear people saying "I don't feel I have a choice". Take a minute to think what work pattern you would do if there were no 'shoulds'.

"This (work-life balance) is not corporate social work. It's a business imperative" Courtney Pratt, CEO of Toronto Hydro

The traditional employee is paid for the time they put in at the office and for turning up to fulfil certain responsibilities. You, however, aren't interested in getting paid for face time in the office. That's what caused the stress to begin with. So sell your knowledge, not your time.

How do you do this?

■ **Define your goal.** What do you want? Part time work? A different shift pattern? To sell your services back to the company as a contractor?

■ **Know your boss's needs.** Find out what your boss's needs are and how you can fulfil them. If you do what he needs, then he isn't going to care whether you work at home or are only in the office part time.

■ **Show the benefits**. Make it clear what results you can get for your boss by doing things your way. Point out the additional benefits this will bring him and your colleagues.

The big question for you to answer is "what's important to your boss and your colleagues?" Then, if you can do your job in three days why do you need to be in for five? So long as your colleagues and boss are sold the idea that you can solve their problems for them equally well through your new work schedule, then they are going to be ok with whatever degree of flexibility you need.

Be a great negotiator by selling your results not the length of time you put in at the office.

5.4

Be a career juggler

If you have always worked in one job for one employer, it doesn't mean that you have to carry on that way. Sometimes stress isn't caused by working too much but by doing too much of only one thing. If you are using only one skill and feeling unfulfilled, it might be right to consider a portfolio career.

The portfolio career is an idea conceived by the writer Charles Handy. He suggested that instead of having one career then changing to another one you can use different skills and have different careers at the same time. The variety may bring you a greater sense of fulfilment and balance in your life. There are lots of different ways you can have a portfolio career. You could keep your existing job, reducing the number of days, and take on another part time job using different skills

case study Indira had always wanted to be an actress but worked for years for the government doing a nine-to-five administrative job. At the age of 35 she decided she wasn't willing to keep treating acting as a hobby. However, she was worried about money if she stopped working five days a week.

but earning similar money. Or you might want to do one main job and occasionally do other contracts in which you try out new skills, or perhaps voluntary work.

Or you might earn most of your money from one job and have less money but receiving more career satisfaction from doing one or two other jobs on the side. Here's how it can work:

■ You earn 80% of your salary from job no 1 and get 20% satisfaction.
■ From jobs 2 and 3 you earn 20% of your salary but get 80% satisfaction.
■ You end up with 100% of the same salary and 100% satisfaction.

Portfolio careers can be applied to a whole range of areas of expertise. They give you opportunities to be flexible and also to address new challenges and grow and develop in your career. They also stop you getting stale, bored or over-stressed by one career and with any luck avoid the office politics of being five days a week in one office.

Think about your working week in terms of the time you have available. What strengths do you want to use and what do you want to achieve in this time?

Portfolio careers allow you to be flexible and develop interests in new ways.

Then she found out that her employer would pay almost the same salary as she was currently earning if she worked three days but on an evening shift. When she changed shift she was able to free up time to take on some real acting jobs and also take a course in art, which she had long wanted to do.

5.5

Trust your instinct

Many people will say that instinct is illogical and doesn't belong in a business setting. However, there is a lot of evidence showing that top business people make some of their best decisions based on intuition and instinct rather than logic. This is as true for career decisions as in any other business decisions.

For years intuition has been dismissed as inferior to logic because instinct is 'just a feeling'. Malcolm Gladwell in his bestseller *Blink* showed how valuable intuition can be. Some scientists say that it is the result of our clever brains putting thousands of pieces of information together incredibly quickly to come up with conclusions. This all happens in millions of parts of a second to give us that sudden feeling that leads to an 'ah ha' intuition. Some people get a physical feeling in their stomach or solar plexus. Others have a thought coming out of nowhere into their head or an image floating into their awareness.

■ **What is your intuition telling you?** Take a look at your vision. Now instead of relying on logic, what does your instinct say? Many people try to force a career plan because it looks good on paper even though something nags away inside telling them it doesn't feel quite right.

"I rely far more on gut instinct than researching huge amounts of statistics" **Richard Branson, founder of Virgin Group**

■ **Logic must be balanced with intuition.** If someone overrides their intuition with logic they may make strides in their career but then reach a sticking point where they lose interest. If they had balanced their logic with their intuition they would have avoided going down the wrong track.

■ **Intuition needs to be exercised.** The most successful business people use their logic and intuition in partnership. Intuition is like a muscle you need to exercise all the time by noticing when you listen to it and your resulting decisions pay off. Everyone experiences intuition in their own way and a positive intuition may be different from a negative intuition, so learn to recognize yours.

Intuition is of course just a starting point. Once you are aware of your instincts, then start asking questions. If your instinct tells you its time for a change, then take the risk.

Exercise your intuition to make sure your career vision is both logical and feels instinctively right.

Change your career

If you aren't satisfied with what you are doing, then perhaps you need to make a radical change. Do you want a new job in the same industry, or perhaps the same kind of role that you currently have but in a different sector?

6.1

Be flexible

Having a positive outlook to change will carry you through any challenges while looking for a new job. Human beings face huge amount of changes in their lives. Your ability to handle change has an enormous impact not just on your emotional well-being but also on how effective you are when looking for a job.

Some people love the challenge of new experiences. Others hate the loss of familiar ways of doing things.

If you can handle change then you will be able to stay the course for longer, have more energy and enthusiasm, and come across better to potential employers.

one minute wonder Give yourself a new routine, even if it is artificial. Draw up a new schedule for the next few weeks and months even if it includes non-work related stuff like going to the gym. Write down time you will use for research, networking and other job-related activities.

Many people become very anxious at the thought of change. They stay in one job far past the point where they should have made a change and miss out on opportunities for promotion or to develop themselves as people. Why?

■ **People like routines.** Many, if not most, people love routines. They like having a clear identity. When asked what they do, they reply simply with a job title. They like knowing where they should be and what tasks they need to do on a daily basis. For many employees, what they do each day to earn a living is what gives them a feeling of self worth and confidence in their abilities.

■ **But resistance to change is damaging.** Change is part of life. People who fight it can spiral down into a series of negative feelings until some structure is restored. This can be the same whether you leave a job voluntarily or because you are forced to. According to research, the negative emotions generated by resisting change may include shock, denial, anger and depression. If, on the other hand, you accept change quickly, then you can take control of your own destiny.

■ **Be prepared to change your routines.** Being flexible and ready for change will keep you in control. Manage change as soon as you see it coming by letting go of the old routines quickly. Put in place new routines and structures as soon as possible. Instead of resisting change and going through all the unpleasant emotions described above, put your energy towards fulfilling your goals and personal sense of purpose in work and life in general.

Instead of trying to resist change, put new routines and structures into your life as soon as possible.

6.2

Open up your options

If you have been working in one organization for a long time, you may have been very narrowly focused on your job and limited your opportunities without realizing. Now is your big chance to sit back and look at what other options and opportunities might be out there and perhaps have a go at something totally different.

When you decide it might be time to change your career, the one person you can count on is yourself. Life has a habit of throwing us unexpected changes and it is what we do with them that makes all the difference. If you are good at numeracy in one job, you are not going to suddenly stop being good with numbers if you change jobs. Likewise, if you have been a fantastic leader for 10 years, you will probably continue to be so for the next 10 or 20 years. Take some simple steps to open up opportunities.

1 Revisit your career vision and goals. It might be that you always had a career change in mind as a goal or you might need to rethink some of them.

2 Revisit your CV. Your skills and experience are transferable. Now is your chance to harness these skills and look for new opportunities to use them in a different setting.

3 You might want to think about particular areas of interest you have never pursued before or perhaps a new job that didn't exist when you started your career. You might want to turn one of your hobbies into a career.

4 Remember, you are the designer of your own destiny. You don't have to do what you have always done. You can totally reinvent your career at any time.

Think creatively. Every year new jobs are created globally, partly through the growth in new technologies and the internet. Web designers, online journalists and bloggers are 21st-century professions. If these jobs didn't exist in your childhood or in your parents' generation, think what other professions might exist even within the next 10 years or so.

Are you open enough to new opportunities to see them and grab them when they appear?

Be alert to new forms of work that have been created in the 21st century.

6.3

Plan your campaign

You can't expect to make a successful career change through luck alone. Planning always lies behind any successful career move. Thoroughly defining the type of role, organization and sector you want to work in makes the difference between ending up in any old job and a career in which you can really grow.

There are a few easy to follow tips for making sure you don't waste time doing unnecessary research and instead keep focused on achieving what you want in the minimum time possible.

Start by writing down all your options. It's no point doing your research then a month later adding what you could have thought about to begin with. Start big, then narrow down. What sectors? What companies within those sectors and what roles within those companies?

one minute wonder Write out a network contacts list. Who do you know already who might have links to the sort of organization you want to work in? Remember that networking is great for getting referrals to future work possibilities.

If you set some clear criteria you can start cutting out as well as adding companies. Here are some of the things to think about:

■ **Size.** How big or small a company do you want to work for? Think about the culture and feel of your ideal company.

■ **Location.** Where would your ideal company be located? Would you rather have a short commute or a pleasant location? In the town or the country?

■ **Culture.** What would be the culture of your ideal organization? A well-established company or market leader, or a new or start up environment?

■ **Activities.** What are the activities you would do in your ideal role? What wouldn't you do?

■ **Colleagues.** What about your boss and the other members of the team? What would be the ideal style of the people you want to work with?

These sort of questions will let you narrow down your options and you will probably end up with a few organizations, and maybe one or two roles that are front runners for your attention. Then you can sit down and really do your research and narrow down your options even further. The more you research different organizations, through networking, or desk-based research, the clearer you will get about your ideal organization.

You are most likely to hit a bull's eye if you aim at it rather than everything on the board.

6.4

Keep research records

Once you have your target job and organization clear in your mind, it's time to get out there and meet people to gather information and hopefully get an interview (and a job offer). It's all going to be much easier and more structured if you keep good records of what you have done so far and what's left to do.

It doesn't really matter whether you design a fancy spreadsheet or keep papers in a folder. The key is to think of career change as a business campaign. For a good campaign you need to be able to track what you have done, what you know, what has worked, what hasn't worked and what you might do differently next time:

■ **Records of contacts.** The sort of things you are going to want to keep a note of include your target companies and any key contacts within those companies along with their contact details. Also keep a note of which of them you have contacted, when and what was the result of the contact. If any of these contacts link up, make sure you note down which person referred you to another contact.

one minute wonder Take the time to write down all your reasons for targeting a particular company and sector. This will drive how you approach contacts and the sort of information you ask for and also help you to tailor your CV to your target market.

■ **Recruitment agencies.** Also keep a record of any agencies and search firms you are in touch with. The quality of recruiters can vary, so it is good if you can track the effectiveness of the company or particular person in getting you leads.

■ **Current industry news.** It is also useful to keep a record of the information you find out about your chosen industry. Do you know what current trends are affecting your sector? Who is doing well and who isn't? What are the critical issues for your industry? This will help you to identify gaps in your knowledge and to develop questions for neworking meetings and interviews.

■ **Useful resources.** Finally, what about useful databases and sources of information? Tap your contacts for resources that you can draw on. It is great to have an on-going list of useful books, websites and databases, even links to magazine or newspaper articles that you can refer to again if needed.

Keep your records up-to-date. Add to them, use them and be more focused on your target.

Keeping records will stop you wasting time and energy when job-hunting.

6.5

Buy a coffee

When you are looking for a new job, ask your contacts to refer you to people they know who might be able to help. Offer your referrals a coffee, and use your short meeting over the coffee break to gather information about your chosen career path.

Asking people directly for jobs doesn't usually work. It is very unlikely that the people you ask will have the right job for you, and also they will feel uncomfortable if they feel 'sold to' or pressurized by you. On the other hand, people are generally willing to help if you ask for a small amount of time and a small amount of help.

■ **Start with your existing contacts.** As soon as you start looking for a job, ask your existing group of contacts whether they know anyone who might be able to help you do your research and find out more about the general area or type of organization you might look for. You'll probably be given several names of people who might know some broad aspect of what you are looking for.

"Feel the fear and do it anyway" Author Susan Jeffers

one minute wonder End your quick meeting by asking if there is anyone else your referral thinks could help you even more. Most people when asked will come up with the name of other contacts they can refer you on to. In the short time it's taken you to drink a coffee, you have grown your network.

■ **Regard your referral as a mentor.** Any name you're given is a 'referral' with whom you can ask to meet. The best people for you to be referred to would be in your chosen area or using similar skills: someone who could be a mentor in the industry, a good networker or a person who is able to give you general objective advice on recruiters, your CV, interviews or the relevance of your skills and experience.

■ **Ask for a short meeting with your referral.** Most people have time for a cup of coffee. When you contact your referral, ask them if you can ask questions about their work and buy them a cup of coffee in exchange. Use your time efficiently during this brief meeting. Ask for any information you need about people, organizations or your chosen profession. You will be surprised at how happy the majority of people are to help in these small ways.

In each information-gathering meeting you have the opportunity to sell yourself in a way that creates interest and leads to new contacts.

Make use of referrals. You can get a lot of answers in the duration of a coffee break.

6.6

Prepare for interviews

An interview might consist of anything from a quick chat and a nod that you've been given the job to a highly structured series of meetings with a panel of people. However, all types of interview can be conquered if you follow these tips.

■ **Do some research.** Find out about the company before you get there. Look at their website, learn about their customers and competition. This will give you genuine questions to ask in the interview.

■ **Prepare questions.** How much do you know about the lines of responsibility in the job, the culture, your daily routines and how success will be measured? Ask if you aren't sure.

■ **Review your CV.** Many candidates are caught out on their own CVs. They forget what they wrote (which is why it's good to be honest). Can you talk about your skills and achievements with confidence?

■ **Bring your CV.** Don't assume your interviewer is prepared. Bring copies of your CV and a notebook to take notes. It's ok to bring a list of questions too. It looks efficient and is.

■ **Dress for success.** Choose the same style as other people in your industry but dress smartly even if others are casual. Wear what makes you feel confident and people will treat you as if you are.

one minute wonder Always send an email or letter as a follow up after an interview. It's a reminder to the interviewer of you and what you might bring to their company. Just write a simple thank you for the time they gave you, followed by "I look forward to hearing from you in due course." This is a last chance for some marketing.

■ **Be punctual.** It's such a simple thing, but turning up late can lose you the interview even if you have everything else going for you. Look up your route in advance and get there 10 to 15 minutes early.

■ **Practice confidence.** Just before the interview think about a time when you felt very confident in the past and imagine that you are there again. This 'anchors' the feelings and makes you feel confident now.

■ **Show motivation.** People want to employ you for your enthusiasm as well as knowledge. Get yourself into a good state before the interview by thinking about why you will enjoy the job.

■ **Use your elevator pitch.** Most interviews start with a question like "tell me about yourself". Here's your chance to introduce the important things about yourself within a couple of minutes.

■ **Remember to listen.** A successful interview will be a 50/50 conversation between you and the interviewer. Listen and let them talk too. They need to sell their company to you as well.

An interview starts the moment you walk into the reception, so be prepared.

6.7

Be memorable and likeable

When you try to change career, you will start meeting a lot of new people: some through networking and 15-minute meetings, others through interviews. It's a competitive world out there. You will be treading the same path as your competitors, so how do you make sure that you are the candidate who stands out in a positive way? The key is rapport.

Rapport is the secret to being likeable and memorable (in a good way). Rapport is that feeling of chemistry you can get when you meet someone for the first time.

■ **Seeing rapport.** You can see if you are in rapport with another person, or a group of people, because you sit or stand in a similar way to them. Your posture may be the same. You may catch yourself making similar gestures or having your arms and legs in the same position. For example, you are cross legged with your arms on the seat rest; so is the other person.

one minute wonder Video yourself. It's a great preparation for interviews. If you don't know what you look like talking about yourself film yourself introducing yourself. Time yourself. If you talk for more than a couple of minutes, cut your pitch.

■ **Hearing rapport.** You can also hear rapport. You may catch each other using similar words or jargon; you start talking at the same pace or volume. Perhaps you find that you even change your accent slightly to sound more like the other person.

■ **Matching and mirroring.** These actions of rapport are known as matching and mirroring. They tend to happen subconsciously, but you can also learn to do them deliberately. If you match body language, words or voice characteristics and start to feel rapport, then they've worked. You know you are in rapport when you think: "this person is just like me", or just feel synchronized with them in some way.

■ **Avoiding mimicry.** However, be careful not to mimic the other person. The difference between mimicry and matching and mirroring means changing your behaviour too much within the other person's conscious awareness. If you mimic, then you will be memorable in all the wrong ways: instead of thinking what a wonderful person you might be to employ, your interviewer is more likely to think how bizarre you are!

Matching and mirroring are actions that build rapport and leave the interviewer with a good impression.

6.8

Know your fit

There are infinite numbers of questions you could be asked at interview. However, you can put most of them under one title: 'fit'. The big question that an employer really wants answered is whether you are going to fit in with the job and the organization. Coincidentally, this is the same question that you, as the career changer, want answered as well.

The first type of fit focuses on **job fit**: i.e. skills and experience and motivation.
■ Can you do the job?
■ Have you the necessary knowledge and years under your belt?
■ Do you have the necessary functional or technical skills?
■ Can you show that you will stay satisfied in this type of role?

one minute wonder Think back to your past roles. How many of your jobs ended because of bad job fit and how many because of bad culture fit? What do you need to know for your next job?

Be prepared to give evidence of what you can do. Sometimes, interviewers will ask you to describe a situation in which you have demonstrated key skills (known in jargon as competencies) or they will describe a scenario and ask you how you might handle it.

In either case think about past achievements and what skills these required. You can use these as a touchstone for what you could do in future. Then be really clear about your motivation for wanting this job using these skills. You must be able to articulate why you want something as clearly as what you want.

The second type of question tends to focus on **organization or culture fit**: i.e. compatibility with the company's way of doing things, its beliefs and values.

■ Are you going to fit in with the team?
■ Do you dress like other people in the organization?
■ Are you someone who would be ok to chat to on a daily basis or go for a cup of coffee with?

This may not sound as important as job knowledge, but studies show the biggest contributors to job and employee dissatisfaction is culture fit. If you don't see your working environment in the same way as other people you work with, then you're going to find it very difficult to get on with people and will end up either leaving or being fired. But in a job of the right fit, it will make you stay when the going gets tough.

Make sure you know your fit with the organization's needs in terms of skills and culture.

6.9

Get ready for green

Skilled negotiators get the jobs they want. Whenever you talk to someone who might be able to give you a job, be ready for signs of interest from the interviewer. If you get 'green signals' it is a sign that the negotiating power is running in your favour and the interviewer is seriously considering you.

Any negotiation between two parties is a powerplay between what you each have to sell and what you each want to buy from the other person.

■ The interviewer wants someone to do the job and is offering a salary and career progression.

one minute wonder Salary discussions: Until you get those green signals don't talk money. If the interviewer tries to introduce the subject you can say something like, "I am sure that your company has very fair remuneration; if we have a good match I am sure we will be able to agree on salary".

■ You want a job and are offering your skills and experience in return for a suitable fee.

■ During an interview, each of you tries to work out if there is a sell/buy match. Whoever wants more at each stage of the interview has more power.

The positive turning point in any such discussion comes when the person stops questioning and starts to try to 'sell' to you by talking about how wonderful the organization is, or how great the facilities are, what a fantastic bunch of people these are to work with or what a great career you could have here.

Other 'green signals' that you can look out for are:

■ When the interviewer starts talking about the job as if you were already in it. They might say something like "when you are running this department..." This shows that they have already got a picture in their mind of having successfully employed you.

■ Or, when they give you a tour of the building – even better if they show you where you might work.

■ Or, if the interview goes on longer than originally scheduled, take this as a positive.

■ The same goes if the interviewer asks for a follow-up meeting with your future team or brings in someone else unexpectedly into the room to meet you. This is a sign that they are taking the opportunity to seek approval from the people who count.

When you see a green signal, respond quickly to keep the interview in your favour.

Go it alone

For some people self-employ-ment comes as a result of redundancy or retirement. Others decide to go it alone in order to have flexibility or to make money directly as a result of the energy they put in on a daily basis. What-ever the route you choose, there are some secrets you need to know if you want to make a success of self-employment.

7.1

Have passion and a plan

Probably one of the reasons you are considering being self-employed is to have more time, or more control over what you do, so you can be more yourself or do things your way. Make sure you have a clear plan and the passion to see it through.

It's rather sad that many people who become self-employed don't make money as easily or quickly as they thought and so they make compromises, and their motivation immediately starts seeping away. The passion disappears from their career. Of course you need to make money, but this should not be at the expense of your passions or you might as well go back to employment again.

one minute wonder Ask yourself: what do I want my business to look like by this time next year? Then ask yourself: in five years' time what would my business need to look like for me to know I have been successful? Jot down anything that you think of and build your plan from there.

> **"Choose a job you love and you will never have to work a day in your life"** Confucius

There are two ways round this conundrum.

1 First of all make sure you really want the route you are taking before you start down it. It's no point being half-hearted about self-employment. You could end up working harder to earn money than you did when you were employed. You need to have a real passion for whatever you set out to achieve.

2 Secondly, plan, prepare and think things through. If you leap in without thinking, you might be lucky but then again you might not. Align your personal and business goals. What's the focus of your business? When do you aim to turn a profit? What kind of business is it going to be? What makes you ready to do this now?

You may change your plan as you go along but it's your goals and your motivation to achieve them that are going to keep you going. If you have a plan and passion, you aren't going to have to fake it with clients and that's the best marketing tool you have. If you can market well, then you have the start of a great business.

Revisit your personal goals and align them with your business goals.

7.2

Be a detail person

Many people who become self-employed become so carried away with their business idea that they forget to look at the administrative detail. But the administration is just as important as the more glamorous sounding parts of the business.

You may have the greatest product or service on the market but find you leak away your profit by not keeping your eye on the day to day running of the business.

Most self-employed people tend to be better at one aspect of administration than another. The entrepreneur who is great at marketing may not be good at filing, for example. The businessperson who is a fantastic book-keeper may not be creative or innovative about new products and keeping ahead of the competition.

You need to make yourself really clear about your strengths and weaknesses in handling the background detail of running a business.

■ **Identify the gaps in your skills.** How much genuine experience have you had with accounts, administration, liaison, IT, etc?

one minute wonder Lots of first-time businesses fail when they aren't thought through. Jot down some ideas to stop this happening to you in answer to these questions: What are the factors that could cause my business to fail in the first year? What about the longer term? What are my risks?

■ **Do you need to hire anyone?** If you aren't naturally great at the detail side, then employ someone who is. Get yourself a part-time secretary and an accountant. If you can't afford or don't want full-time employees, then just pay someone to freelance when you need them.

■ **Get quotes.** If you have a one-off project that needs doing, or even a regular piece of work, get quotes from different freelancers. There are lots of creative self-employed people out there just like you who need the work and will do a quality job.

■ **Don't just look locally.** You can hire people as remotely as you want. For some tasks nowadays, you don't even need to use someone in the same country as you. I know people who have hired workers based overseas at a tenth of the rate they would pay in their own country.

Whatever you do, make sure you keep good accounts and keep a watchful eye on your cash flow and how the business is going. It would be a shame if you created a great product and won customers, but ended up with no business because you had overlooked the detail.

Don't be afraid to hire people to help you out, it will save you money in the long run.

7.3

Fix your fee

It's one thing to complain about the salary you are receiving from your current employer and quite a different thing to consider your potential value in the marketplace. When you are preparing for self-employment, it is vital to work out your salary expectations and how to fulfil them.

1 First of all, think about what you currently earn. Don't just think of your basic salary. What about all the hidden extras: pension payments, bonuses, any contributions to housing, travel? It is worth writing a long list and ticking off all those that you would need to maintain of you were self-employed.

2 Then think about what you expect and want to earn. Are you prepared to take a salary cut to compensate for the freedom of being self-employed? Would you sacrifice in the short term for longer term gains? Or perhaps you are expecting to earn far more as a self-employed person than as an employee.

3 Look at your market. You may want to earn this amount but how much do your potential customers expect to pay? Your customers may expect to buy in cheap services in your field, especially if there are a lot of people competing for the same custom.

4 If you are selling a product rather than a service, make sure you sensibly price your product to take account of all associated expenses and overheads as well as your own cut.

5 What about *how* you charge? Deciding to set an hourly or day rate, or fee per service or other unit can made a big difference to your earnings potential.

6 Make sure you understand how taxation works for the self-employed, or you could end up with far less than expected.

Once you have determined your relative worth, decide on a rate and stick with it. This will ensure that you negotiate strongly with clients and maintain your brand in the market.

Know your worth and set a fee that reflects your brand in the marketplace.

7.4

Be on the web

Entrepreneurs need to keep on top of their game and be open to new ways of building and marketing their business. The internet opens up all sorts of opportunities for any size of business to compete in every market in the world.

A well-designed website lets you reach out to existing customers and keep your existing ones happy. Whether you are working by yourself or have your own business employing other people, it's worth creating a website to promote what you have to sell.

Whatever your business you will have competitors. If you want to stand out from the crowd you need to get your name out there and be seen and talked about. The great thing about a business website is that you don't need to be in the same street, town or even country as your customers. If you are selling a good service or product, you can be in China and they can be in India, but potentially they will find you.

one minute wonder Think about creating a regular online or email newsletter for your customers. This can be a very effective method of marketing. However, make sure the content has useful tips and freebies, not just advertising.

There are a few important points to bear in mind:

■ Do you need help to build a site? With a moderate level of computer know-how, it is possible to build a simple website and be up and running within a matter of hours. However, unless you have an advanced understanding of the technicalities of e-commerce and search engine optimization, as well as a flair for design, then you will probably want to hire specialists to build a truly effective site for your business.

■ Know your cyber-audience. Whether you build your own site, or employ others to do so, you need to have a clear vision of who you want to appeal to. Are you aiming to sell online or is the website a handy information board about you? How will you attract your customers back again and again?

■ Beware good looks at the expense of practicalities. Some website designers create great looking sites, with slideshows and animations, but they accidentally mask the more basic elements needed by search engines – indeed, some of the flashiest sites are virtually invisible on web searches. Make sure you consider the search engine factor *before* you or someone else starts building your website.

Focusing your website on a particular audience will help you come up with an effective marketing plan and stop you wasting time and money on something that might look wonderful but never be used to its full potential.

Creating a professional, well-focused website will help to build your business.

7.5

Count your cash

You aren't going to get rich the moment you become self-employed unless you have an amazing idea that you sell to a friendly billionaire on Day One. If you work for yourself there are going to be times you aren't earning and times when you earn a lot, so good money management is the key.

Getting over-excited when your first cheque comes in and blowing the lot isn't going to make you successful in self-employment. The difference between working for yourself and working for someone else is that those cheques don't always come with the same nice numbers on every month. What's more, you've got lots of business expenses as well as yourself to pay.

one minute wonder Ask yourself: What money do I expect to make? What money do I need to make to cover my expenses? How soon will my business break even?

■ **Feast and famine.** Sometimes you are flooded with work and the profits are rolling in. Then all at once business grinds to halt and the orders, work and profit stops and you don't know where your next cheque is going to arrive from. Then there are costs to take care of.

■ **Remember the tax element.** You may not be paying tax regularly anymore, so you need to keep track of how much of the money coming in actually belongs to you rather than to the government. Every number coming in and out of the business needs to be thought about and spent wisely.

■ **Factor in the downtimes.** Are you likely to work during holiday periods? What other downtimes might there be for your business? What money do you need to keep back to cover the lean periods? Remember you can't eat and house yourself on trust of future business; you need to have a bit of fat for the lean times as well.

■ **Open a business account.** It's worth having a separate account for your business. Work out what to deposit for the basics of the business before calculating what you can afford to pay yourself. Once you have an effective cash flow system, stick to it scrupulously. Charting your income flow will help you keep a visual eye on what's going on.

Open a separate business account and manage your money well from the first day of self-employment.

7.6

Define your target market

When you become self-employed, you will need to become a salesperson whether you like it or not, and you will need to know the market you are selling to inside out. It's the same whether you are offering products or services, and whatever sector you are in.

It's amazing how many people become self-employed without thinking about the basics of marketing. Yet if you don't sell, you don't eat. It's a very basic sum – how well I market is directly related to how much money I earn.

Now, if you are very lucky you may open your office door and accidentally trip over some generous clients. If you are normal though, you need to think about who is going to buy from you, and that means having a business plan.

You don't need to sit down and be an accountant, but there are some simple questions you need to ask of yourself.

■ **Product.** What sort of service / product am I offering and who is likely to want this product and why?

■ **Price.** What price will make me a profit? How does this compare with the price of my competitors?

■ **Competition.** Who else is selling this and why would people buy from me rather than them? What distinguishes me in a positive way? Do I need to do research?

■ **Location.** Where am I going to be located and is this the same place that my potential market is? Is this the best location?

■ **Promotion.** What methods will I use to market myself? Who am I targeting? What will persuade them to buy from me?

Understanding your product and target market will make sure that you win the right customers and develop a clear place in the market for what you are selling. This is the same whether you are selling the same single job as when you were employed or whether you are starting up a business with the hope of expanding and adding employees.

Update your marketing strategy regularly to make sure you know your own business and to stay ahead of the competition.

7.7

Be great with people

Some people have very poor people skills. If they are already employed, then they might hang on to their job despite this deficiency. However this is not a strategy that works for the self-employed. It's always important to have good interpersonal skills if you want to progress in your career, no matter what sector you're in.

Once you are out on your own you need to be able to handle clients. Even if you decide to get someone to market your business for you, you will probably need some client skills and certainly management skills. If you decide to sell your services as a freelancer, every piece of work you get will come indirectly or directly as a result of your interpersonal skills. Here are some of the reasons why you are going to need good people skills:

■ You will need to be your own sales and marketing person.
■ You will have to negotiate terms with clients and suppliers.
■ You may have to deal with staff as an employer.
■ You definitely need to be a great networker.
■ You need to encourage people to pay you on time.

"Seek first to understand"

Steven R Covey, author of Principle-Centred Leadership

If you aren't good at handling rejection or conflict, think twice about becoming self-employed. Will you be able to deal with being turned down for work as a freelance again and again? However good you are at what you do, your product or service won't suit everyone, so you need to be able to bounce back.

Remember there are going to be times when you will be criticized for not delivering exactly what the client wanted even if your clients are lovely people. Moreover, some clients may not be nice at all, so how are you going to deal with difficult customers when you have done nothing wrong, or dealing with suppliers who haven't delivered on time?

As you can see, you will need great communication and people skills to be self-employed. If you do have these then you have the beginnings of a great career.

Develop your communication and interpersonal skills so you can handle a variety of situations.

7.8

Have a contract

Not everyone in business believes in the phrase "my word is my bond". In fact, some businesses will try to encourage you to put in extra hours for the promise of a reward that never comes or the old lie "the cheque is in the post". Many self-employed find this out too late to their cost.

It's not good to be too cynical about human nature, but some people aren't as nice as others in business. After all, the goal of most businesses is to turn a profit, and profit should be your goal as well. If you don't make money your business will soon cease to exist. This does not mean you have to give up ethical practice.

False promises come in the form of lures to the sole trader or small business:

one minute wonder Don't put all your eggs in one basket: clients come and go and you can't rely that your business will always attract the same clients again and again. Set a limit of a maximum of 25% of turnover from one client.

"You give this to me for free and you will win the job eventually."

"You can't charge for those extra hours because I will find someone else who can do the job cheaper."

"Oh, didn't I say that expenses weren't included?"

■ **Make a proper contract.** There's only one way to make sure you are in the best position possible and that's to have a solid contract for everything to do. It will make sure that you are properly compensated for all the hours you put in unless you agree up front that you will give something away for free.

■ **What to include in the contract.** Your contract should have everything you have negotiated in it, what results you will get and for what money, hours and expenses including what your client will supply and what you will supply. If you are selling a physical product, you need to think about what will happen if delivery is delayed. If you are going to be paid in stages, think about exactly what you will supply at each stage.

Of course your client may choose not to honour your contract but then you can choose what consequences to apply. Start self-employment in a business-like fashion and you will have a far higher chance of long-term career success.

A contract is a safety net that protects both you and the client.

7.9

Be resilient and persistent

Success in self-employment doesn't always come quickly and it doesn't always happen in a straight line. There will be times when everything seems to be going smoothly and periods when you don't seem to be making much progress at all. If you are not self-motivated and resilient, it's going to be tough.

It's sometimes said that it takes two years for someone to get used to being self-employed. In reality you can adapt much more quickly than that if you accept early on that you are in charge and whatever happens you can cope with it.

■ **Keep learning.** While being resilient is partly down to your character it also helps if you stay on top of your profession. In an employed job, the company will pay to keep you trained up and ahead of the competition. In your own business, however, you are the only one who can give yourself new skills. If you can motivate yourself to keep learning, you will have an extra edge when times get tough.

one minute wonder Do a regular review. Ask yourself, what worked well today / this week? Is there anything I need to do differently? Is there anything I can learn? Making this a habit will help you to grow and develop and do the same for your business.

■ **Remember your goals.** But the real secret of resilience goes back to goals. When you know what you want to achieve and you have really thought your vision through in detail, you are much more likely to stick out the tough times because of the reward that will one day follow.
■ **It's all down to you.** When you work for yourself, there is no one to make you get up in the morning and do what needs to be done. There is no one to tell you how to organize your time or deliver on time. You need to have the motivation every day to manage your time and get your work done by the deadline.

Can you hold yourself accountable for the tasks that need to be done? Can you keep motivated even when it would be easy to be lazy and forget working for a few days? If you can honestly answer 'yes' then you are right for self-employment.

Keep yourself accountable for working hard and focusing on success every day.

Jargon buster

Assessment centre
Formal interview or development situation where you are assessed for your skills and attributes.

Bereavement curve
The theory that we go through a series of emotions when a big change like redundancy occurs, before settling into acceptance.

Board interview
Interview where there is more than one interviewer in a panel or board.

Body language
How you communicate through your facial expressions, gestures, posture and voice rather than words.

Brand
How you define what you do in your career so people recognize your unique qualities.

Career chapters
The roles you have held throughout your career. Look back at these for clues to job satisfaction.

CAR format
Challenge, Action, Result formula for achievements (see also STAR format).

Career transition
Also called Outplacement – a service to help you find another job and gain related skills, particularly used during redundancy.

Competency
A skill or strength you demonstrate in a work environment.

Competency-based interview
Interview focusing on examples of what you have done and what skills you have demonstrated as a result.

Elevator pitch
Short speech in which you sell yourself to a future or current colleague or employer.

Headhunter
Recruitment agent generally specializing in higher end jobs.

MBTI/ Myers Briggs
One of the most popular psychometrics (see below).

Networking
Talking with a purpose to get industry knowledge, visibility or contacts.

Psychometric
Questionnaire / tool for showing you your strengths, abilities and behaviours.

Referral
A contact that you can follow up to get meetings or information.

Six degrees of separation

Theory that we are all separated from anyone else in the world by just six links. Used in networking.

STAR format

Used to work out achievements. A Situation or Task, the Action you took and the Result you got.

USP / unique selling point

What makes you stand out from your competitors (marketing term).

Viral marketing

Use of word of mouth to spread news about a new product.

Further reading

Bannatyne, Duncan *Wake Up and Change Your Life* (Orion, 2009) ISBN 978-0752882871

Bolles, Richard Nelson *What Color is Your Parachute?: A Practical Manual for Job-Hunters and Career Changers* (Ten Speed Press, annual) ISBN 978-1580089319

Boyes, Carolyn *Cool Careers* (Harper Collins, 2008) ISBN 978-0007263523

Bridges, William *Creating You and Co.: Be the Boss of Your Own Career* (Nicholas Brealey, 1997) ISBN 978-1857881547

Bridges, William *Jobshift: How To Prosper In A Workplace Without Jobs* (Da Capo, 1995) ISBN 978-0201489330

Conner, Daryl *Managing at the Speed of Change: How Resiliant Managers Succeed and Prosper Where Others Fail* (Villard Books, 2006) ISBN 978-0679406846

Eggert, Max *Perfect CV* (Random House, 2007) ISBN 978-1905211739

Eggert, Max *Perfect Interview* (Random House, 2007) ISBN 978-1905211746

Eikleberry, Carol *The Career Guide for Creative and Unconventional People* (Ten Speed Press, 1999) ISBN 978-1580080750

Handy, Charles *The Hungry Spirit: Beyond Capitalism – A Quest for Purpose in the Modern World* (Arrow, 1998) ISBN 978-0099227724

Keirsey, David and Bates, Marilyn *Please Understand Me* (Prometheus Nemesis, 1984) ISBN 978-0960695409

Saltzman, Amy *Downshifting: Reinventing Success on a Slower Track* (Harper Business, 1992) ISBN 978-0060921583

Sher, Barbara with Glottieb, Anne *Wishcraft: How to Get What You Really Want* (Ballantine, 2003) ISBN 978-0345465184

Tieger, Paul and Barron-Teiger, Barbara *Do What You Are: Discover the Perfect Career for You Through the Secrets of Personality Type* (Sphere, 2007) ISBN 978-0316167260

Useful websites

www.monster.com – one of the largest jobs websites

www.learndirect.gov.uk – UK government website that is a useful source of information about work and learning

www.idf50.co.uk – aimed at people aged 50 or over with links and information including international

www.jobsetc.gc.ca – Canadian government website with employment advice and job bank

www.seek.com.au – Australian employment and recruitment site

www.shlgroup.com – Saville and Holdsworth site with sample psychometrics and tests

www.worktrain.gov.uk – government national jobs and learning website offering training and career change information and a jobs database

www.youreable.com – provides information for people with disabilities

www.prospects.ac.uk – UK official university graduate career website

www.careerage.com – English-language Indian website with careers advice and jobs in South Asia and the Middle East

www.careersa-z.co.uk – information on individual careers and training

www.careers-portal.co.uk – UK government site on careers choices

www.humanmetrics.com – information on psychometrics

www.BusinessSecrets.net